MIRACLES

——— FROM THE ———

FINGERTIPS of GOD

THE POTTER

DAVID ROMERO

WESTBOW
PRESS®
A DIVISION OF THOMAS NELSON
& ZONDERVAN

WestBow Press books may be ordered through booksellers or by contacting:

WestBow Press
A Division of Thomas Nelson & Zondervan
1663 Liberty Drive
Bloomington, IN 47403
www.westbowpress.com
1 (866) 928-1240

Scripture taken from the King James Version of the Bible.

All scripture quotations are from the King James Version unless otherwise noted

ISBN: 978-1-9736-8759-7 (sc)
ISBN: 978-1-9736-8758-0 (hc)
ISBN: 978-1-9736-8760-3 (e)

Library of Congress Control Number: 2020904669

Print information available on the last page.

WestBow Press rev. date: 04/07/2020

CONTENTS

DEDICATION

I would like to dedicate this book to the following three people.

First: To my wife Sheila of 53 plus years for the patience and support she has provided. Without her love and care none of this book would be possible. She has been my most valuable source inspiration.

Second: Robert Duhon a very good friend from high school and fellow believer in Jesus Christ. He was both encouraging with his kind words and monetary investment.

Third: A special character, JJ Jasper. As a busy radio personality, speaker and author, he not only answered my email requesting his thoughts of the rough draft; he spent his valuable time doing just that and added a few other ideas in the mix.

A very special thanks to the three of you!

THE POTTER

My prayer is that all who read this book will come away with a better understanding of how much God loves us and to what depth He has gone to that we might understand that.

> Thus saith the LORD, thy redeemer, and he that formed thee from the womb, I am the LORD that maketh all things; that stretcheth forth the heavens alone; that spreadeth abroad the earth by myself. (Isaiah 44:24)

On the pottery wheel, with my dirty hands in the clay, God revealed His personal love for me. Just as He did with Jeremiah, God gave me a revelation through the scriptures of Jeremiah 18:1–6 of His desire to remake me into His personally handcrafted image. The image of His Son, Jesus, "that maketh all things," without guilt of sin, came to His creation and got His hands dirty with the process of salvation. He did that so all of us who believe would be remade and reconnected in the relationship Adam originally had with the Father.

INTRODUCTION

This Is God's Analogy

The word which came to Jeremiah from the LORD, saying, Arise, and go down to the potter's house, and there I will cause thee to hear my words. Then I went down to the potter's house, and, behold, he wrought a work on the wheels. And the vessel that he made of clay was marred in the hand of the potter: so he made it again another vessel, as seemed good to the potter to make it. Then the word of the LORD came to me, saying, O house of Israel, cannot I do with you as this potter? saith the LORD. Behold, as the clay is in the potter's hand, so are ye in mine hand, O house of Israel.

—Jeremiah 18:1–6

In this revelation, Jeremiah is called to the potter's house to see the clay being worked. The vessel he saw being formed was marred. Then Jeremiah witnessed the potter reworking the vessel. In verse 11, God instructs Jeremiah to go and speak to the men of Judah:

"Now therefore go to, speak to the men of Judah, and to the inhabitants of Jerusalem, saying, Thus saith the LORD; Behold, I frame evil against you, and devise a device against you: return ye now everyone from his evil way, and make your ways and your doings good." For Judah, at that point, it was not too late. God was allowing them a last chance to repent. And with His hands and their obedience, He would remake them into a holy nation.

This picture is as true for us today as it was for the men of Judah in that day. Much time has passed, and in today's extension of His creation, He warns us to repent in order to avert His judgment in the same way He warned the men of Judah.

In verse 12, they refuse God's warning: "And they said, There is no hope: but we will walk after our own devices, and we will every one do the imagination of his evil heart." Let us take heed and learn from their choice while time permits. Let us repent and avert a soon-to-come judgment.

Let us take a closer look at God's analogy and how it compares to the actual process of making pottery.

I started making pottery in 1969. With that hands-on experience and the revelation of God's Word, the Holy Spirit enabled me to see deeper into His analogy. Hopefully, I can point out those parallels from the book of Jeremiah and other parts of the Bible so you can see what I see.

Pottery is a craft that many people are familiar with today. It has somewhat of a mysterious ability to draw people in when they observe the process in action. Before Jeremiah's day, until a few centuries ago, it was a craft that supported civilization on a daily basis. The potter and his shop were absolute necessities in most communities. Today it has been relegated to an artistic craft.

Manufacturing technology has replaced the handcrafted vessel with the inexpensive and almost valueless containers we see on the market shelves today.

In the natural, four elements are necessary to do pottery, and there are four primary parallels to the analogy in the supernatural.

Natural Elements and Their Spiritual Parallels

The potter: a human in the natural
God the Father: the Master CraftsmanGod the Father, Creator of humankind, is the Potter in this analogy.

Water: a created substance
Jesus: mediator between God and humankindJesus is the mediator. God planned a reconnection between Himself and humankind.

Clay: a created substance
Human: the "Substance Hoped for"
Humans, as the clay, need the touch of God upon their lives to be complete.

Step-by-step process
The Holy Spirit: facilitator of the processThe Holy Spirit is our hands-on teacher and coach. As the Holy Spirit works in our daily lives, He provides the step-by-step process by which God reworks us into worthy vessels.

A person of faith is the only created being who, by God's personal touch, can be reworked, reshaped, and reformed into the likeness of God, the Master Craftsman, as we will see in this comparison.

CHAPTER 1

The Potter:
God the Father, the Master Craftsman

The Potter in this analogy is our sovereign God. The overall picture is one of God pulling humankind up toward their divine destiny, which only God can best see and do. Psalm 8:5 states that we have been made just a little lower than the angels and crowned with glory and honor. A good example of this is Saul. God remade him into the vessel He wanted him to be.

God spoke to Ananias.

Then Ananias answered, Lord, I have heard by many of this man, how much evil he hath done to thy saints at Jerusalem:

And here he hath authority from the chief priests to bind all that call on thy name. But the Lord said unto him, Go thy way: for *he is a chosen vessel unto me, to bear my name* before the Gentiles, and kings, and the children of Israel:

For I will shew him how great things he must suffer for my name's sake.

And Ananias went his way, and entered into the house; and putting his hands on him said, Brother Saul, the Lord, even Jesus, that appeared unto thee in the way as thou camest, hath sent me, that thou mightest receive thy sight, and be filled with the Holy Ghost. (Acts 9:13 emphasis added)

God took Saul and reworked him into Paul, just as Jeremiah saw the potter rework the marred clay into a worthy vessel. God placed His name upon Paul and "sealed him" by His Spirit. He left His mark on him. God has not stopped doing this. He reworks many of us today and seals us by the name of Jesus when we declare ourselves believers.

Potters signature

Hebrews 11:1 says, *"Now faith is the substance of things hoped for, the evidence of things not seen,"* (emphasis added)

I have taken the liberty to use God's Word and work it into the analogy of the potter. It goes like this. By the measure of faith given to us now, we—the substance—place ourselves in the Potter's hands to be formed into evidence of our full potential, which is yet unseen.

Let's expand on these key points.

Faith

The whole quality of our existence relies on this truth: sin made faith necessary. From Adam to the second Adam (Jesus), faith was our connection to God. From Jesus's birth until His Second Coming, faith has been and will continue to be necessary to connect with God. Faith comes by hearing His Word. From the promised Messiah of the Old Testament to our faith in Jesus today, what He did on the cross for all reconnects us to real life, eternal life. When Jesus returns at His Second Coming, faith will have served its purpose and will no longer be necessary.

"Now" Faith

Our God is focused on right now. He is perfect in all His timing. His Word (scripture) gives us the measure of faith necessary for today. He expects us to be obedient to His will. In obedience, we can trust Him to provide for our needs for today. Jesus said this is the way we should pray: "Give us this day, our daily bread" (Matthew 6:11).

If we don't obey, how can we expect God to honor His Word? Faith is retained when obedience is practiced. Our faith accumulates and builds our spiritual beings as we seek and develop our relationship with Him.

Substance

We are the substance God has created and chosen to work with.

> I am the LORD, and there is none else, there is no God beside me: I girded thee, though thou hast not known me:
>
> That they may know from the rising of the sun, and from the west, that there is none beside me. I am the LORD, and there is none else.
>
> I form the light, and create darkness: I make peace, and create evil: I the LORD do all these things.
>
> Drop down, ye heavens, from above, and let the skies pour down righteousness: let the earth open, and let them bring forth salvation, and let righteousness spring up together; I the LORD have created it.
>
> Woe unto him that striveth with his Maker! *Let the potsherd strive with the potsherds of the earth. Shall the clay say to him that fashioneth it, What makest thou?* Or thy work, He hath no hands? (Isaiah 45:5 emphasis added)

Our Creator made us from a substance He created—earth—which He spoke into existence. Humans are the only created beings God made with His own hands, in the same way a potter shapes and forms a vessel. By faith we have the ability to be remolded and remade into the original plan He had for you and me. We are a workable substance, teachable in all His ways. Through faith and obedience, He seeks our compliance in His perfectly talented hands.

In submission to His will, the Holy Spirit proceeds to do a work in us comparable to the way a potter works clay. We should trust the one who can do the work necessary to bring us to the point of fullness in Christ. Within our own human abilities, we are not able to do this.

Only with the Spirit of God alive and working in us can we ever approach the point of our full, God-given potential. He created this potential in us at conception and, quite possibly, into Adam himself, who bore the seed of all humankind.

Evidence

Relationship is a process that provides hope for His perfect will to manifest in our lives. The Word of God is alive and sharper than a two-edged sword. By way of His Spirit living in us, He convicts us of sin, and this brings us to a point where we must choose to deal with it or not. Before salvation, we are hindered by the flesh to deal with our sins. Our original nature is the sin nature, which leads us to more sin and eventually death. Only by faith and through the blood of Jesus can we grow into our full potential, into salvation. He builds His purpose into us to contain and demonstrate His image and talented glory.

Unseen

Sanctification is the process that guides us, by the Holy Spirit, to bring the development of our potential to a point of maturity in Christ. At salvation, what we call the rebirth, our spirits are made perfect in Him. However, the flesh and the soul are not. At this point, the Holy Spirit is given access to our flesh and minds by the blood of Jesus. The process of sanctification begins. It's a continuous one that lasts until we breathe our last breaths. His grace and mercy are always available to us by prayer and by the Holy Spirit acting in our spiritual interests. He looks upon the depth of our hearts.

Throughout this analogy, you may catch some repeated observations and comparisons. On the potter's wheel, a piece of clay will undergo hundreds of revolutions before the master is satisfied with its beauty and function. Likewise, repetition of the truth in the Word helps us retain the image of His Son.

Only He can always see one's full potential. At times, it may be obvious to all. In comparison, He grows us in the knowledge of the Word, which contains all His promises to us. The Holy Spirit, with His guiding skill, reworks our lives into the image of Jesus. Sometimes the change and growth is quick.

God the Father chooses to communicate with us in ways we can understand. God is a Spirit, but He describes Himself in human terms. In this analogy, He is the potter to both Jeremiah and to us. He is the one in control.

> My Father, which gave them me, is greater than all; and *no man is able to pluck them out of my Father's hand.* (John 10:29 emphasis added)

We must understand that we are made in His image by His own Word.

> Let us make man into our likeness and Image. (Genesis 1:27)

God describes Himself in terms we can relate to. In Deuteronomy 33:27, He speaks of His arms that uphold. In Joshua 10:29 and Isaiah 66:2, He speaks of His hands, and in Isaiah 66:1, He speaks of the earth as His footstool, implying He has feet and legs.

The process of making pottery is a beautiful analogy of God and humans in relationship with each other. It's an image that is functionally understandable. By using the analogy of the potter and the clay, God paints a picture we can all see, understand, and most of all, experience by faith through His gentle touch.

The Potter's Hands

At times we can feel the hands of God on our lives. The hand is often used to demonstrate authority. As Father and Creator, His authority certainly should be without challenge. Here His hands convey and demonstrate His love and care as only He can.

He is the source of all authority—absolute and unconditional. It is His wish that we choose to submit to His authority through His Son Jesus.

> For as the Father hath life in himself; so hath he given to the Son to have life in himself; And hath given him authority to execute judgment also, because he is the Son of man. (John 5:26)

As the source of all authority, the Father delegates His authority to His Son Jesus, the Son of Man. *Authority* is defined as the right to do or not to do because of position or office; the legality.

There are two basic types of authority: intrinsic authority and derived authority.

Intrinsic authority refers to one's essential nature. This can be demonstrated in both positive and negative ways. God's love evokes positivity and hope, while His judgment seems to be very negative—at least for those in its direct path. Even evil people possess intrinsic authority. For instance, dictators rule from a source of fear. Even from such an evil source comes a degree of order within the bounds of this authority. Our Father is the ultimate source of all authority. The potter possesses this authority over the clay as we see in Isaiah 45:9.

Derived authority is received from another source. Jesus gets His authority from the Father. The authority under which Jesus acted was directly from the Father. He stated many times that He did as the Father directed. This can be seen in many scriptures, such as John 12:50, 14:31, and 15:9.

As we will see in the next section of the analogy, the hand of the potter works only through the use of water to form the clay into a useful vessel. In this same way, the hand of God cannot rework us except through our faith in Jesus, the living water. We see a more complete picture of this later in the analogy.

As Jesus's authority came from the Father, the source of our authority is derived directly from the blood covenant we have with Jesus. Our God-given authority is too vast to discuss here. Know this: If this authority is not put into practice, it is lost by default. The loss is not permanent; it merely goes into a state of atrophy, like an unused muscle. When we obey, we allow the Father, the craftsman potter, to move us, the clay, closer to our full potential, to the image of His Son Jesus, the anointed one.

We will either have faith in what has been sacrificed for us, or not. With applied faith, comes promises of life, in abundance. If we are found without faith, that which we have will be stripped away.

> For unto everyone that hath shall be given, and he shall have abundance: but from him that hath not shall be taken away even that which he hath. And cast ye the unprofitable servant into outer darkness: there shall be weeping and gnashing of teeth. (Matthew 25:29–30)

We have all been created to have the potential of full relationship with the Father. Sin has marred the created material, humankind. Again, it's His intention to rework us into our full potential by our faith in what Jesus did for us on the cross. His authority comes to us with love and gifts. Someday we will have to account for whether or not we allowed Him to apply His authority to our lives.

Jesus said it this way in Luke 12:48:

> But he that knew not, and did commit things worthy of stripes, shall be beaten with few stripes. *For unto whomsoever much is given, of him shall be much required*: and to whom men have committed much, of him they will ask the more. (emphasis added)

God Uses His Authority to Reshape Our Lives

The potter has total authority to mold, shape, and remake the pot into whatever He chooses in order to serve His purposes. His vision, as sovereign God, sees what is best for each of us. Our problem is learning to trust His vision instead of our own.

The authority we experience comes directly through the touch of God upon our lives. Examples of this are governments, parents, the church, and employ.

Our governments and institutions have derived authority given by God. Even in the republic we live, we relegate our God-given authority to a group of representatives elected to act on our behalf to serve the nation, state, municipality, and individuals.

Within the church, God ordained a structure built around the fivefold ministry.

Within the family, He ordained a structure in which the husband is the head of the household.

> "For the husband is the head of the wife, even as Christ is the head of the church: and he is the saviour of the body" (Ephesians 5:23).

When we hear the Word of God, a seed of faith is planted and begins to take root. It establishes a root of knowledge, creating a desire for more. As this process is repeated, the practice of hearing and believing grows our spirit man to higher levels of faith and knowledge. Consequently, it grows our relationship with the Father while learning to trust the touch of His hand.

> The word which came to Jeremiah from the LORD, saying, Arise, and go down to the potter's house,

and there I will cause thee to hear my words. Then I went down to the potter's house, and, behold, he wrought a work on the wheels. And the vessel that he made of clay was *marred* in the hand of the potter: *so he made it again* another vessel, *as seemed good to the potter* to make it. (Jeremiah 18:1–4; emphasis added)

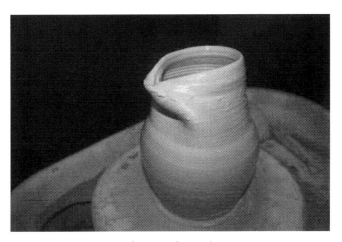

A marred vessel

"So He made it again." Being born again is as if we are being created as a new vessel, this time with His own Spirit, "as seems good to the potter."

We are each made once and born into sin. The master potter made a way by which we can be remade into a suitable vessel worthy of His love and craftsmanship.

In John 14:6, Jesus said, "I am the way." The way was made possible totally by His authority and perfect will for each of us. We have to hear the Word, act on the faith it imparts, and then believe and trust His hand upon our life.

As a new creature in Christ, the following is how He reworks us. Restoration: He builds us back up to our unseen potential.

> He restoreth my soul: He leadeth me in the paths of righteousness for His Names sake. (Psalm 23:3)

We are remade in His image to demonstrate His love for us and others.

> Brethren, if a man be overtaken in a fault, ye which are spiritual, restore such an one in the spirit of meekness; considering thyself, lest thou also be tempted. Bear ye one another's burdens, and so fulfil the law of Christ. (Galatians 6:1–2)

As He restores us, we are to likewise restore others. Throughout His Word, He demonstrates His perfect love for us. As His vessel, we hardly ever stand alone. When we stand with other believers, we are all made to display a greater image of who He is.

By our faith in Jesus, we invite the Potter to take us apart individually and restore us to a spiritual state of righteousness using His omnipotent hands and by His loving ways.

> A time to kill, and a time to heal; a time to break down, and *a time to build up.* (Ecclesiastes 3:3; emphasis added)

Develop: He grows us in skill and knowledge.

I will run the way of thy commandments, when thou shalt enlarge my heart. Teach me, O LORD, the way of thy statutes; and I shall keep it unto the end. (Psalm 119:32–33)

In His Word, our God promises to give us life and to give it in abundance. Through our faith in Him, His Word works to expand and establish our faith to greater levels. Once more, by our faith, He works into us a higher degree of sophistication and continues the process of maturing our characters in the spirit of who He is.

Redirect: He puts us back on His path.

In all thy ways acknowledge him, and He shall direct thy path. (Proverbs 3:6)

Our flesh will sometimes continue to hold on to parts of our old, dead sin nature even after we have obtained a degree of maturity in Him. The Holy Spirit works through the process of sanctification to continually clean up our lives by the cleansing power of the Word. When we get off center with Him, He quickly pulls us back in line to the degree we cooperate. We will see a better picture of this in chapter 4, where the clay has to be centered before the potter can work it.

In the same way a potter centers clay, the living Word wants to bring us to a formable potential where we can be in balance and aligned with Him. It's an ongoing process we go through daily. Round and round on the wheel: "Line upon line, line upon line, precept upon precept, precept upon precept" on the true wheel of the potter.

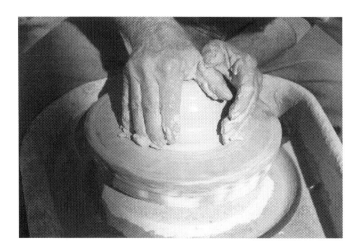

Wheel work centering

O Lord, I know that the way of man is not in himself: It is not in man that walketh to direct his steps. O Lord, correct me, but with judgment; not in thine anger lest thy bring me to nothing. (Jeremiah 10:23–24)

With His hand on our lives and by faith through grace, we place our trust in the Father's vision. He is faithful to make us into the vessels of His desire. He is our designer and Creator, who builds His purposes uniquely within us. He applies His Word directly through His touch on our spirits and flesh. Yielding daily, He remakes us into worthy vessels as a result of the righteousness of His Son Jesus. The more we see ourselves growing righteously by His touch, the more trust develops, giving us rest in His loving hands.

Purpose: He sees us in His likeness and image.

So God created Man in his own image, in the
image of God created He him; male and female
created He them. (Genesis 1:27)

He set out to do this intentionally. By His design and in His
image we are made. We exist as unique patterns and designs
created for the purpose of bringing us into His divine fellowship.
Through the first Adam's disobedience, the sin nature entered
in and marred man, keeping him from reaching his God-given
potential and removing him from direct relationship with the
Father.

Through salvation and sanctification provided by the second
Adam, God reclaims His marred creation and works it back into
a worthy vessel. His desire is focused on us. His love provides the
way for our restorations. Likewise, God has created in us a desire
for a relationship with Him and others. That desire comes from
the image and likeness of who He is. When His Spirit is alive in
us, it draws us to Him. He wants us to choose Him in the same
way we like others to choose us. We are a "chosen" generation.

His handiwork can truly be seen in us.

Photo of a group of pots

CHAPTER 1 REVIEW

Our Father in heaven has a designed destiny for each of us. In Jeremiah 18:6, He says, "cannot I do with you as this potter? saith the LORD. Behold, as the clay is in the potter's hand, so are ye in mine hand."

Our trust has to be in the one who uniquely formed us. God says His ways are higher than our ways. God instructs Jeremiah to go to the potter's house to see an image that helps communicate a picture of what He wants him to see. Sin has damaged us. In the eyes of our minds and the windows of our souls, God wants us to see how much He loves us and wants to restore us back to our original design.

In the same way our Father worked in covenant with His chosen people Israel, He works with us. His blood covenant gives Him total authority to remake us, His body (bride), just as He did the nation of Israel. In a like manner, He rebuilds us individually to the degree we obey and allow Him to do the work.

Just as the potter can bring down a piece of marred clay, so does our Father allow us to fall to a point where He can bring us back up in a manner that will glorify His divine nature. Remember, we are made in His image and likeness. When Adam sinned, humankind's image was severely marred and not worthy of relationship with Him.

As creatures with free will, by faith in the Master, we yield ourselves to His hand for the process of being remade worthy.

My attempt to express the beyond description desire the Father has to touch us and develop a close relationship is shabby at best.

The Creator and controller of the universe desires to relate to a mere speck of dust in the vastness of all He created.

> And the LORD God formed man of the dust of the ground, and breathed into his nostrils the breath of life; and man became a living soul. (Genesis 2:7)

Selah! Think about that!

His desire is a hands-on relationship with each and every one of us in the same way a potter works on a wheel and desires each piece to be his or her very best.

CHAPTER 2

Water, Substance:
Jesus, the Mediator between
God and Humankind

Jesus Christ is our mediator between the Father and all humankind.

Jesus answered and said unto her, If thou knewest the gift of God, and who it is that saith to thee, Give me to drink; thou wouldest have asked of him, and he would have given thee living water. The woman saith unto him, Sir, thou hast nothing to draw with, and the well is deep: from whence then hast thou that living water? Art thou greater than our father Jacob, which gave us the well, and drank thereof himself, and his children, and his cattle? Jesus answered and said unto her, Whosoever drinketh of this water shall thirst again: *But whosoever drinketh of the water that I shall give him shall never thirst;*

but the water that I shall give him shall be in him a well of water springing up into everlasting life. (John 4:10–14; emphasis added)

He that believeth on me, as the scripture hath said, out of his belly shall flow rivers of living water. (John 7:38)

To work clay successfully on the wheel, the potter must use water as a lubricant between the clay and his or her hands. In this analogy, God has provided Jesus to be the mediator between Himself and us. John 14:6 tells us, "Jesus said 'am the way.'" Jesus Christ, the Son of God, is the living water our Father, the potter, chose to deliver His grace and mercy to the clay of humankind.

Jesus is the one who removes the friction of life in the flesh. He replaces it with living water, which allows the hand of God to move and make us as He would. His desire is a smooth and trusting relationship between Himself and His creation, humankind.

The process by which pottery is made has been practiced since almost the beginning of time. Only in most recent times has the knowledge and importance of this process begun to be lost because of efficient technology. Automation has changed it from a necessary functional craft to almost only an artistic venture. Throughout time, the potter has chosen individual pieces to represent not only the function of his or her craft but its aesthetic side.

The analogy illustrates to observers and students of creation the fact that our God has made us in a wonderful way. It also shares with us elements of His talents, grace, and mercy.

But now, O LORD, *thou art our father; we are the clay, and thou our potter; and we all are the work of thy hand.* (Isaiah 64:8; emphasis added)

Jesus Facilitates Our Contact with the Father

His blood covenant, another picture of a living liquid, is the conduit for the grace and mercy of God to do the essential work of salvation in our lives.

> For we have not an high priest which cannot be touched with the feeling of our infirmities; but was in all points tempted like as we are, yet without sin. Let us therefore come boldly unto the throne of grace, that we may obtain mercy, and find grace to help in time of need. (Hebrews 4:15–16)

Just as water is necessary between the hand and the lump of clay, so is Jesus necessary between the hand of the Father and His children.

We know Jesus walked the earth as both God and man. This picture will be seen again in chapter 4, when we see how the water worked with the clay becomes both water and clay over time. In pottery, this result is called slip.

Paul says it this way: "To whom God would make known what is the riches of the glory of this mystery among the Gentiles; *which is Christ in you, the hope of glory*" (Colossians 1:27; emphasis added).

Jesus is the river of living water flowing from God the Father to us through His blood covenant. As God, He is one with the Father. As our Savior, He is one with us.

In the latter stages of throwing on the wheel, the water becomes one with the clay, slip. Then progressively, some of the slip becomes one with the pot.

As the potter's hands cannot work the clay without water, in the same manner, God cannot work on us directly without Jesus, the bearer of His grace and mercy. He comes by our invitation through faith in Him, unlocking the way to the Father. Jesus said in John 14:6, "I am the Way the Truth and the Life: no Man cometh to the Father but buy me." Moses did not have the access to the Father that we have today through Jesus.

> And he said, Thou canst not see my face: for there shall no man see me, and live. And the LORD said, Behold, there is a place by me, and thou shalt stand upon a rock: And it shall come to pass, while my glory passeth by, that I will put thee in a clift of the rock, and will cover thee with my hand while I pass by: And I will take away mine hand, and thou shalt see my back parts: but my face shall not be seen. (Exodus 33:20–23)

If God our Father were to touch humankind, the substance of His creation, without His grace and mercy first having been applied by faith in Jesus, humankind would be totally destroyed. Again, clay cannot be worked on the wheel without water. It must be applied to reduce the friction between the hands of the potter and the clay. Likewise, one must first have salvation by faith in Jesus Christ before the sanctification process, *remaking*, can begin.

And the Lord said unto Moses, depart and go up hence, thou and the people thou hast brought out of the land of Egypt, unto the land which I sware unto Abraham, to Issac and unto Jacob, saying, Unto thy seed will I give it: And I will send an angel before thee; and I will drive out the Cannanite, the Amorite, and the Hittite, and the Perizzite, the Hivite, and the Jebusite. (Exodus 33:1–2)

Here, the angel sent out is the "Spirit of Grace."

Unto a land flowing with milk and honey: for I will not go up in the midst of thee; for thou art a stiff necked people: lest I consume thee in the way. (Exodus 33:3)

Like the potter's hand on the clay without water, God's righteousness upon man would consume him without first being forgiven. In Exodus 33:3 He says, "I will not go up in the midst of thee … lest I consume thee." The blood Jesus shed for us is the medium of forgiveness God uses between His hand and us, the clay. He is truly our source of living water.

And when the people heard these evil tidings, they mourned: and no man did put on his ornaments.

For the Lord had said unto Moses, say unto the children of Israel, Ye are a stiffnecked people: I will come up in the midst of thee in a moment, and consume thee: therefore now put off thy ornaments from thee, that I may know what to do unto thee. (Exodus 33:4–5)

As we will see in chapter 3, clay can be too stiff and, therefore, too difficult to work. Just as clay has to be pliable and moldable, we, the substance, have to yield and be willing to be formed into God's perfect will for our lives.

> And the children of Israel stripped themselves of their ornaments by the mount Horeb. And Moses took the tabernacle and pitched it without the camp, afar off from the camp, and called it the Tabernacle of the congregation. And it came to pass, that everyone which sought the LORD went out unto the tabernacle of the congregation, which was without the camp. (Exodus 33:6–7)

Moses, knowing the people, as an extra measure of precaution, chooses to place the tabernacle away from the camp. In the next sentence, Moses indicates that perhaps not all of them sought the Lord.

> And it came to pass, when Moses went out unto the tabernacle, that all the people rose up, and stood every man at his tent door, and looked after Moses, until he was gone into the tabernacle. (Exodus 33:8)

Moses here and throughout his life is a type and shadow of Jesus. He was the mediator for these stiff-necked people just as Jesus is a mediator today for all believers.

And it came to pass, as Moses entered into the
tabernacle, the cloudy pillar descended, and stood
at the door of the tabernacle, and the LORD talked
with Moses. (Exodus 33:9)

Like Jesus, Moses, by his faith, had direct and personal
communication with the Father.

And all the people saw the cloudy pillar stand at
the tabernacle door: and all the people rose up
and worshiped, every man in his tent door. And
the Lord spake unto Moses face to face, as a man
speaketh unto his friend. And he turned again into
the camp: but his servant Joshua, the son of Nun,
a young man, departed not out of the tabernacle.
(Exodus 33:10–11)

Moses, like Adam in the garden, spoke to God face-to-face.
Joshua, in preparation for his leadership role, hungered for more
interaction with his God.

And Moses said unto the LORD, See, thou sayest
unto me, Bring up this people: and thou hast not
let me know whom thou wilt send with me. Yet
thou hast said, I know thee by name, and thou hast
also found grace in my sight. Now therefore, I pray
thee, if I have found grace in thy sight, shew me
now thy way, that I may know thee, that I may find
grace in thy sight: and consider that this nation is

thy people. And he said, My presence shall go with thee, and I will give thee rest. (Exodus 12–14)

The grace of our God is always present with all believers. His grace provides rest and peace in times of trouble.

And he said unto him, If thy presence go not with me, carry us not up hence. For wherein shall it be known here that I and thy people have found grace in thy sight? Is it not in that thou goest with us? So shall we be separated, I and thy people, from all the people that are upon the face of the earth. (Exodus 33:15–16)

We are all familiar with the time line. God walked with humans in the garden until they sinned. Up to that point, humans were in fellowship with God daily. Once sin entered the picture by the humans' own choosing, it marred direct contact and made it no longer possible.

But we are all as an unclean thing, and all our righteousnesses are as filthy rags; and we all do fade as a leaf; and our iniquities, like the wind, have taken us away. And there is none that calleth upon thy name, that stirreth up himself to take hold of thee: for thou hast hid thy face from us, and hast consumed us, because of our iniquities. (Isaiah 64:6–7)

When Jesus completed God's plan by offering His life upon

the cross, He reestablished the path to fellowship with the Father. When we, as believers, accept His offering, we are given access to the Father and to newness of life.

> Jesus said unto her, I am the resurrection, and the life: he that believeth in me, though he were dead, yet shall he live: And whosoever liveth and believeth in me shall never die. Believest thou this? (John 11:25–26)

In Jeremiah 18:1–10 the story is one of Israel being called to repentance. In Romans 6:16–18, Paul says it this way:

> Know ye not, that to whom ye yield yourselves servants to obey, his servants ye are to whom ye obey; whether of sin unto death, or of obedience unto righteousness? But God be thanked, that ye were the servants of sin, but ye have obeyed from the heart that form of doctrine which was delivered you. Being then made free from sin, ye became the servants of righteousness

Jesus is the way by which the potter, our Father, remakes us, His vessel.

As stated in Jeremiah 18:4, "And the vessel that he made of clay was marred in the hand of the potter: so he made it again another vessel, as seemed good to the potter to make it."

A marred pot

We Are Remade into His Righteousness, Reflecting His Likeness and Image

The following is a true story of the pot that returned home. It is very similar to the parable of the prodigal son, which many of us know well.

The hundreds of pots I made in the twenty-five years I worked with clay were either sold or given to someone who admired them. Some were made to be gifts. Many my wife lived with like they were children, and when we considered them grown, and not having enough space in our home, we allowed them to move out and find another home. But each one had a special place in our hearts.

In my last year of college, my senior show consisted of 120 pieces on display, and I had just begun. This was January 1970.

One day, a couple of years ago, my oldest daughter, Monica, called and said, "Daddy, I have something I want you to see. I was at this flea market, just looking around, when this pot caught my eye. So I walked over to check it out. As I got closer, I knew it was one of your pots."

Later, she brought it home for me to examine. The moment I saw it, there was no question. You never forget one of your own.

I want you to know God knows every one of His creations. He knows you better than you know yourself. Now, to continue with the story.I turned the pot over, and sure enough, my name was scratched on the bottom with the date, August 30, 1970. I always sign and date my work.

He is waiting for you to place your faith in His Son Jesus. By that faith, He places His mark on you. Never to be forgotten! Continuing again.

Monica was only two and a half years old when this pot originally joined our family. At some later date, it had grown up and moved away under circumstances I don't remember.

Monica said, "Daddy I just couldn't leave it there. They were asking eighteen dollars for it, so I paid the price and took it home."

God will not just leave you where you are! He has paid the price for you with the blood of His Son, and He wants to take you home. Now tell me, isn't that just like a true father? No matter how long you've been gone, God pays the price so we can find our way home. Still more.

I was just beginning the process of preparing this teaching when this happened. I have seen God's hand at work many times and in many ways using the talent He placed in me. It seems as though God has been preparing this incident for a very long time. Before Monica left that day, I could see the parallel of this event to the parable of the prodigal son. The pot remains with me to this day as a reminder of the price God paid for my redemption. A picture of the prodigal pot follows.

The prodigal pot

CHAPTER 2 REVIEW

Clay on the wheel cannot be worked without water between it and the potter's hands. Water serves as a lubricant, reducing friction between both. This analogy is a picture of and a direct parallel to how Jesus is the mediator between the Father and you and me.

God has made Jesus His provision for us. Jesus tells us in John 14:6, "I am the way." Jesus Christ, the Son of God, is the living water, which our Father, the potter, chose to deliver His grace and mercy to the clay of humankind.

> I am the Way the Truth and the Life: no Man cometh to the Father but buy me. (John 14:6)

Jesus came to the earth to establish Himself as our Savior/mediator. In doing so, He came as both God and man. When water and clay are mixed in the process of doing pottery, it becomes slip. For that short time when Jesus hung on the cross and took upon Himself the sin of humankind, it was as if the clay and water had mixed. At that point, the Father could not look upon His Son because of the sin He bore on our behalf. The water and clay had become, in comparison, slip. It was then that Jesus became the penalty of disobedient and sinful humankind, so we could have access to His Spirit by faith.

Jesus provided the source of personal relationship, which had been lost by Adam in the garden. Jesus provided His righteousness through His death and resurrection. Our faith in Jesus unites us in a spiritual exchange of our righteousness for His. When the Father looks on a believer, He sees the person clothed in the righteousness of His Son. Again, this illustrates the point of how similar the clay being absorbed into the water is to how our Father establishes us firmly into the finished work of Jesus, the living water.

As in the personal story I recounted, the Father wants us to be in His presence for all eternity. He offers us adoption into His family for an everlasting relationship. We are His handiwork, His vessels for various use, all displaying His perfect talent and desire. Do we want to cooperate with His will?

CHAPTER 3

Clay, Substance:
Humans: the Substance Hoped For

These are the liberties I've taken with Hebrews 11:1: "*Now faith is the substance of things hoped for, the evidence of things not seen*" (emphasis added).

By the measure of faith given us now, our God is a right now God.

We, the substance, place ourselves in the Potter's hands to be formed. Through obedience and trust, we allow Him to form us into the evidence of our full potential, which is still unseen.

The good potter seeks a workable material suitable for His intended purpose.

Humans are the substance God created and chose to use for His purposes. Like clay selected by the potter for its potential, God selects us as His material of choice for the potential He sees in us. Not just as individuals but also corporately, as two or more.

God sees the potential we contain and the contributions we can make to His purposes.

Unlike clay, we can choose to jump off the wheel through free will. We can refuse to allow the hand of God to guide our growth into a vessel worthy of His image and likeness.

The Touch of God We Feel on Our Lives Is the Potter's Hand

In the previous chapter we discussed how, as believers, God's hand works through His Spirit directly with our bodies and minds.

God said,

> Then He answered and spake unto me, saying, This is the word of The Lord unto Zerubbabel, saying, Not by *might, nor by power,* but by my Spirit saith the Lord of Host. (Zechariah 4:6; emphasis added)

Through an angel, God tells Zerubbabel that all he has accomplished in works for God has not been by his might or power but through the Spirit of God, working in and through his life. This work was in accordance with the will of God the Father.

It is the same spirit—the Spirit of God—that works in the lives of a born-again believer. He works in the same manner, through His Spirit, to maximize the potential He has placed in us. Through our sins or lack of faith, we can hinder His work. Hope lies in the form of the potential that faith can build in us. The knowledge of who He is, His desire for us, and the love He has for us initiates that building process within our form of hope. He so eagerly wants to perform this work in obedience, combined with faith. He begins to fill the voids of our hope. The form is designed to resemble Jesus. His Word says that Jesus in us is our hope of glory.

Our salvation is a personal one because He personally selected and designed us through His creativity. He selected us to be alive today, not two thousand years ago or two hundred years from today. He selected and designed into each and every one of us a potential and a path to follow in order to make the most of His creative purposes. With our obedient compliance and much grace and mercy, we have the hope of reaching the potential He placed within us.

In the same way a potter selects his or her material, God makes His selection specific to His will for each of us. We are His unique creations.

Much like clay, our flesh comes with built-in flaws derived from the sin nature in our unsaved selves. Desires tugging at our will, habits impossible to break, and corrupt environments constantly flood our beings. These worldly contaminants cause the flesh to be unworkable by God until we yield to the cleansing blood of Jesus Christ. Once we yield totally to Him, He can run us through the sieve of His Word, thereby removing contaminates in our lives and making us a workable substance.

Natural clay has rocks, roots, and other forms of contamination. In the early days, a potter had to take the raw material and prepare it to make it workable. Until the twentieth century, potters dug clay out of the ground, dried it, crushed it down to fine dust, and removed the rocks, roots, and any foreign material that would not contribute to the essence or quality of the basic material. The Holy Spirit works with us in much the same way once we have been born again.

By our total surrender within salvation, we give God the right to break us down to whatever degree He needs in order to remove the things that serve no purpose and may actually hinder our lives. The roots and rocks in our lives are sins, traditions, and addictions that cling to our flesh. Sanctification—the removal of foreign things that do not contribute to our wholeness in Him— occurs through the chastisement of our Father, by conviction of the Holy Spirit, and by instruction in the written, spoken, and living Word. The purpose of this process is to get us to a point we can be remade, become usable, to produce and develop the Potter's original intent for our lives. He placed within us a shape and function according to His desire.

Once the potter sifted the dried clay, he reintroduce water and stored the wet clay, often in large pits dug nearby. A substantial amount of time was allowed for the clay to age and mature. Sometimes one generation prepared and stored different clays for the next.

Without Jesus, we are like clay without water, just dry, crumbly, and dusty material without much potential. Once Jesus is introduced, the dry material—humans—absorbs living water in his or her spirit to produce true life workable in His hands. Only the true potter, God the Father, can make provision for this to happen. Moist clay has good body and is very pliable. It can be molded into a shape or form for utility. Humans, with Jesus, are like clay with the right amount of water. They possess unlimited potential in the hands of the potter.

As the relationship with Jesus develops, there is a progressive degree of the ability to grasp on to faith by hearing the Word.

Simultaneously, trust in Him builds, which is what He wants for us in combination with the things He has already done.

Sometimes the pit we find ourselves in seems deep and dark. And it often feels as though a generation has gone by before He reaches in and pulls us out to rework us. In His perfect timing, He lays claim to us, the material needed for His timely work.

The Word of God is alive and works in us who have been born again into a newness of life. He is the source of true life working in our lives, one on one. His Word spoke all creation into existence. His Word says He formed humankind from the dust as in His analogy with Jeremiah. When He made us in His image, He directly designed creative abilities into us to reflect who He is. The full potential of our individual creativity is there to serve His purpose.

A Good Potter Sees the Clay and Knows the Potential That Lies Within

Lump clay and finished pot

God's Word is quick to set a standard of what is acceptable and what is not. It quickly separates the wheat from the chaff. It dispels darkness with light. God sent His Son, the living Word, to separate His children from evil and death unto Himself, providing them life everlasting.

> For the word of God is quick, and powerful, and sharper than any twoedged sword, piercing even to the dividing asunder of soul and spirit, and of the joints and marrow, and is a discerner of the thoughts and intents of the heart. (Hebrews 4:12)

The Word establishes a standard by which He can measure us and we can measure ourselves. It introduces light into the darkest parts of our inner beings. We choose to cling to the light and conform to its leading or to reject it. Doing so leaves us holding on to the edge of the pit. If we choose to hold on, it may be a while before He reaches down to pick us up and place us back on His wheel. Everything happens in His perfect timing.

The potter uses many tools to cut, trim, and support his or her work. These help bring the work to its full potential.

Bible and clay tools

The printed and spoken Word is designed to fit into the hand of the Holy Spirit to trim and fashion us into vessels that reflect the image and characteristics of Jesus within our own unique designs. The Word trims excess from us, leaving only what is functional toward the application of God's calling for our lives. We discuss the process of trimming more in chapter 4.

Pots that are too thick for their designed function are cumbersome and not easy to work with. The excess weight discourages their frequent use. Likewise, pots that are thin walled may be too fragile to sustain long-term use. If they survive frequent use, they will often be retired or placed on a shelf and used sparingly for fear of breakage. An ideal vessel, skillfully made in the hands of the potter, can be used to its full potential. Thus it delivers to its owner its intended function over a long life of productivity.

Sanctification of the flesh is an ongoing process for us, applied by the Holy Spirit. He teaches and prepares us to be a workable and usable substance in the same way the potter goes through his or her process with the clay.

Some clays are selected for their strength and durability, and others for their beauty and purity. Here are some of the more popular clays used today.

- *Terracotta* is very porous and coarse. It is used to create larger vessels and tiles that serve a function analogous to their very source, the earth.
- *Stoneware* clays are known for strength and are mostly used for functional everyday vessels. These clay bodies often have beauty within their own unique characteristics. Besides strength, minerals found in some of them add distinct patterns of coloration to the finished piece that might require little to no decoration. Most clay bodies have an innate beauty of their own. The beauty of God's creation seems to flow right out of them.
- *Porcelain* is a little more difficult to work and can be very fragile when formed and fired correctly. This white-bodied clay gives the artist a free hand at applying any type of decoration to a completely blank canvas.

God seeks the right substance—a human—to produce a vessel that reflects and magnifies who He is. The potter seeks clay that will reflect his or her skill, talent, and intent in a like manner.

God seeks us, whom He created, to contain His Spirit. Only a righteous vessel can serve as His temple, and only God can do this.

Like clay to the potter, we are chosen by Him. But we must willingly cooperate.

As we discussed in chapter 1, our God has a sovereign right to create anything He wants and for whatever purpose He chooses. Because He is love, He has chosen us to be temples, vessels that contain Him in Spirit and truth.

> For thou art an holy people unto the LORD thy God: the LORD thy God hath choosen thee to be a special people unto himself. Above all people that are upon the face of the earth. The LORD did not set his love upon you, nor choose you, because you were more in number than any people; for you were the fewest of all people. Because the LORD loves you, and because he would keep the oath which he had sworn unto your fathers, hath the LORD brought you out with a mighty hand, and redeemed you out of the house of bondmen, from the hand of Pharaoh king of Egypt. (Deuteronomy 7:6–8)

The Jews were God's chosen people, and the image that God gave to Jeremiah in chapter 18 in the book of Jeremiah, spoke of the Jewish nation. Having said this, John 3:16 says, "For God so loved the world that He gave His only begotten Son, that whosoever believeth in him should not perish, but have everlasting life."

Through our faith in Jesus Christ and the work He did on the cross, we are adopted into His kingdom. We see in 2 Samuel 14:14, 1 Peter 1:17, and several other places in the Bible that He is no respecter of persons. His Word applies to all who believe. Therefore, the image of the Jews that God shows Jeremiah certainly applies to us as well. It vividly portrays the way in which God chooses to work with not only Israel but with all believers. Believers are adopted into His family. In Hebrew times, an adopted child was one who was not only chosen but had the same inheritance as the firstborn.

> For thou art an holy people unto the Lord thy God, and the Lord *hath chosen thee*, to be a peculiar people unto himself, above all the nations that are upon the earth. (Deuteronomy 14:2; emphasis added)

This scripture emphasizes that we, not only the Jews, are a chosen people. We, like a special clay body, are chosen by the Potter to produce a vessel that is peculiar, different from the world's point of view. A vessel that is unique unto Him, chosen to be sanctified, consecrated, and made sacred. Because of His loving choice, we should yield to His divine nature, thereby magnifying His Spirit so others can see the evidence of true life.

Potters often choose to keep a special piece for themselves. Such a piece may be unique and represent a special effort or achievement. Usually, this is a one-of-a-kind success.

Photo of first show pot

God Considers Every Person One of a Kind and Irreplaceable

Psalm 33:12 reads," Blessed is the nation whose God is the LORD: and the people whom he hath chosen for his own inheritance."

As a potter, some of the pieces I made were so unique that I did not want to part with them. I've even tried to duplicate some of these with marginal success. The similarities were sometimes very, very close, but each remained unique unto itself. Many of these special pieces I still have and will keep until my children or grandchildren inherit them. Recent discoveries in DNA confirm our uniqueness from any other individual, past or present. You and I are truly one of a kind.

> I have made a covenant with my chosen, I have
> sworn unto David my servant. (Psalm 89:3)

The Potter made an agreement with His creation. His Word is full of promises, which provide us with His life, eternal life. His pledge provides us the power and authority in His Holy Spirit that transforms us into vessels displaying His love, grace, and mercy. When reworked by His hand, we display and share His characteristics, enabling us to function within His will and by His guidance.

> Henceforth I call you not servants; for the servant knoweth not what his lord doeth: but I have called you friends; for all things that I have heard of my Father I have made known unto you. Ye have not chosen me, but *I have chosen you*, and ordained you, that ye should go and bring forth fruit, and that your fruit should remain: that whatsoever ye shall ask of the Father in my name, he may give it you. (John 15:15; emphasis added)

God makes special efforts to select special, preferred material that would yield an extraordinary crop. He builds us into vessels of His special purpose and utility.

> But the fruit of the Spirit is love, joy, peace, longsuffering, gentleness, goodness, faith, vs Meekness, temperance: against such there is no law. Love, Joy, Peace, Long-suffering, Gentleness, Goodness, Faith, Meekness, Temperance. (Galatians 5:22–23)

Again, the Lord states that we have been chosen for His intended purpose of bringing forth fruit or function in accordance with His perfect will. If we choose not to yield and obey, then the Word in Galatians says we will not inherit God's best.

Now the works of the flesh are manifest, which are these; Adultery, fornication, uncleanness, lasciviousness, Idolatry, witchcraft, hatred, variance, emulations, wrath, strife, seditions, heresies, Envyings, murders, drunkenness, revellings, and such like: of the which I tell you before, as I have also told you in time past, that they which do such things shall not inherit the kingdom of God. (Galatians 5:19–21)

If we allow the good potter to use us and make us as He will, we will yield fruit and function according to His purpose as stated in Galatians 5:22–23.

The Holy Spirit best sums it up this way, through the writing of Paul to the Ephesians.

According as *he hath chosen us* in him before the foundation of the world, that we should be holy and without blame before him in love:

Having *predestinated us unto* the adoption of children by Jesus Christ to himself, according to the good pleasure of his will, To the praise of the glory of his grace, wherein *he hath made us accepted* in the beloved. In whom we have redemption through his blood, the forgiveness of sins, according to the riches of his grace; Wherein he hath abounded toward us in all wisdom and prudence; *Having made known unto us* the mystery of his will, according to his good pleasure *which he hath purposed in himself:*

That in the dispensation of the fulness of times he might gather together in one all things in Christ, both which are in heaven, and which are on earth; even in him: In whom also *we have obtained an inheritance*, being predestinated *according to the purpose of him who worketh all things* after the counsel of his own will: <u>*That we should be to the praise of his glory*</u>. (Ephesians 1:4–12; emphasis added)

He chose us before the foundation of the world by His plan, His hand, and for His purpose.

Good clay is easy to prepare and will cooperate well with the potter's hands. This type of clay is often sought for production shops, where a high number of pots are made in a relatively short time. This type of potter doesn't have the time or desire to spend contending with the clay. Another potter may delight in the challenge.

Difficult clay tests the skill and hand of the potter. It often contains the potential of yielding a more unique and eye-catching vessel. It's as if the substance—believers—were taking God up on His Word when He said, "prove me." In circumstances where we resist the hand of God; we may be creating a basis for our testimony to others.

Clay has to be prepared by kneading either mechanically or by hand, in the same way a baker kneads dough. The kneading process removes hard lumps and air pockets that hinder and challenge the throwing process. If this is not dealt with first or well enough, it certainly challenges the potter's skill.

In the same manner, the Holy Spirit works on us, removing

fleshly pockets of resistance and unconfessed sin. He does this to make us conformable and less resistant to the hand of God. It becomes our choice to cooperate or resist His touch.

> Till we all come in the unity of the faith, and of the knowledge of the Son of God, unto a perfect man, unto the measure of the stature of the fulness of Christ. (Ephesians 4:13)

Thank God He has sent the Holy Spirit, who always has the time, inclination, and patience to work with the raw material we are to Him.

In chapter 4, we will see the step-by-step process used by potter.

CHAPTER 3 REVIEW

Humankind is the substance God has chosen to love and use to glorify His creative skill. His talented hands have created a being who is capable of a relationship with Him as well as serving His other purposes. Like clay selected by the potter for its potential, God selects us as His material of choice to display the potential He designs into each of us. He did this for Himself and for us individually and cumulatively as humans. God specifically created our potential so we could participate, by relationship with Him, to develop His plans here on earth.

Moist clay has good body and is very pliable. It can be molded into a shape with the purpose of utility. Man with Jesus is like clay with the right amount of water; it possesses nearly unlimited potential in the hands of the potter. God seeks the right substance—people—to produce a vessel that will reflect and magnify who He is. In this same way, the potter seeks clay that will reflect his or her skill, talent, and intent. We have been chosen by God specifically for the potential He created in us.

The Potter has made an agreement with His creation. His Word is full of promises, which provide us with a path to true life. Like clay, we have to be cleaned up, born again, adopted into His family. His perfect sacrifice provides for us the power and authority of His Holy Spirit, which transforms us into vessels displaying His love, grace, and mercy. Once we are born again, He starts the process of reworking us like clay on the wheel, resembling the characteristics of Jesus. This is called sanctification, a growth and maturing process. It enables us to function in cooperation with His will.

The Potter has made not only an agreement with His creation as a whole but with us personally. His pledge is to love us in our uniqueness, with all our quirks and impurities. His skill is beyond our abilities to challenge Him, if we cooperate. Our DNA proves we have been made, in fact, one of a kind. His Word says we have been chosen before the foundation of the world was laid.

CHAPTER 4

The Process:
The Holy Spirit, Facilitator of the Process and Hands-On Teacher and Coach

But the Comforter, which is *the Holy Ghost, whom the Father will send* in my name, *he shall teach you all things*, and bring all things to your remembrance, whatsoever I have said unto you.

—John 14:26 (emphasis added)

By the measure of faith given us at salvation, the Holy Spirit begins the process that transforms us from an imperfect substance into His finished work. He is not only a comforter, He is also an instructor who coaches us through the refinement process, turning and turning and turning us into the "substance of things hoped for." The Holy Spirit is the same spirit that raised Christ from the dead. Salvation brings us from our death-bound spirits into a new and eternal lives by our new births. It's much like a spirit or spiritual transplant; our spirit is exchanged for His. However, the process is not over; it has just begun. He teaches us all things in much the same way simple clay can be made into an object of functionality and beauty.

> Be it known unto you all, and to all the people of Israel, that by the name of Jesus Christ of Nazareth, whom ye crucified, whom God raised from the dead, even by him doth this man stand here before you whole. (Acts 4:10)

It is only through our faith in Jesus and the work of the Holy Spirit that we can stand whole before Him. We become whole in newness of life by the Holy Spirit reworking our flesh in cooperation with our faith and the knowledge of His Word. Over time, we grow into our full potential, line by line, precept by precept as we were designed.

> Knowing that Christ being raised from the dead dieth no more; death hath no more dominion over him. Nor does Satan and death have dominion over us. For in that he died, he died unto sin once: but in that he liveth, he liveth unto God. (Romans 6:9–10)

Because He lives, by faith we are able to live in the fullness of His Spirit.

> Wherefore, my brethren, ye also are become dead to the law by the body of Christ; that ye should be

married to another, even to him who is raised from
the dead, that we should bring forth fruit unto God.
(Romans 7:4)

As vessels of honor bring acknowledgment of the potter's skill,
likewise, the fruit we bring forth acknowledges the work He has
done in us.

As I have said previously, no matter how skilled the potter is,
no two pieces are ever alike. This is a testament to the uniqueness
God has created in us. Even though we are very much alike, we
are still very different by His plan and design.

Let's look at the steps of working clay and how each one
parallels the way God works with us.

The Process Begins

The potter works the clay in a close version of the following
sequences. God takes the substance—us—and applies His grace
and mercy by means of our faith in Jesus. Then by His Spirit,
He proceeds to develop and reveal our potential, much like the
following eleven steps. Notice again the close parallels between
us and the clay.

Step 1: Sizing the Ball

The potter selects a piece of clay that represents the size, shape,
and strength of the vessel envisioned. The size is relative to the
overall height and thickness of the intended vessel walls. The
thinner the more fragile the walls, and the higher the vessel can
rise. The opposite is true of thicker walls. The firmness of the clay

and its ability to absorb water determine to what degree the clay can be pushed outward and upward.

In this micro-picture we see the firmness of the clay as being equal to the firmness or strength of our faith. The clay's ability to absorb water is equal to the degree of testing our faith can withstand at any given time. If any clay body is allowed to absorb water too long, it will soften and fail. God does not allow us to be tested beyond the ability He gives us to resist. If we fail, it is by our choice. Thank God His hand is there to catch us when we call out for Him.

God has selected each of us for a particular application based on His design, purpose, and destiny. The Holy Spirit teaches and coaches us through this growth process, much like the potter who knows the clay works it to its full potential. He has designed us to be vessels of honor or of utility. He is no respecter of persons. He loves both.

> And we know that all things work together for good to them that love God, to them who are the called according to his purpose. (Romans 8:28)

A good potter will size the piece of clay he has chosen to work based on the size, shape, and purpose of the vessel he intends to create. In the drying and firing process, clay shrinks anywhere from 10 percent to 25 percent depending on its composition and water content.

Likewise, God knows our shortcomings so well that He applies His grace and mercy in ways that yield a workable material suitable for His use. As we yield ourselves to the master potter, He forms us into the potential He placed in us. Through our obedience, He applies His hands to our individual circumstances and shortcomings, raising up for Himself a vessel worthy of honor. We can become worthy of praise and honor to the Master if we yield.

> For whom he did foreknow, he also did predestinate to be conformed to the image of his Son, that he might be the firstborn among many brethren. (Romans 8:29)

As the potter looks at the clay and imagines its potential, our Creator looks at us and sees the end from the beginning. He is more than able to work and rework us, over time, into our spiritual completeness.

> Moreover whom he did predestinate, them he also called: and whom he called, them he also justified: and whom he justified, them he also glorified. (Romans 8:30)

In salvation, we become justified through faith in Jesus, our mediator. We become acceptable for Him to begin the hands-on work we need.

> What shall we then say to these things? If God be for us, who can be against us? (Romans 8:31)

Yielding to the hands of the Master, they become all-encompassing as our sources of protection, direction, strength, and uplifting,

He that spared not his own Son, but delivered him
up for us all, how shall he not with him also freely
give us all things? (Romans 8:32)

The potter selects and pays for the clay either monetarily or by
the sweat of his or her brow.

Our master has not only created us; but, has redeemed us at a
great cost. Tell me, what greater honor is there for us than to be
bought and paid for by the Son of God.

Step 2: Secure the Clay to the Wheel Head

The portion of clay is literally slapped onto the wheel head by
the potter to ensure a secure bond between the two. Depending
on the size and firmness of the clay, much strength may need to
be exerted for the clay to be worked into shape. If the clay is not
securely bonded to the wheel head, the clay may fly off the wheel,
requiring the process to be restarted.

Numerous times Jesus said, "Follow me." How well we adhere
to the Rock of our salvation, Jesus, the living Word, determines
how quickly and effectively the Holy Spirit can do His work in us.
By developing our faith through the knowledge of God's Word—
line upon line, precept upon precept—He anchors us securely in
our salvation. A well-developed faith helps ensure that no matter
how much force is exerted upon us by worldly circumstances, or
by the chastisement of the Father Himself, the Holy Spirit will
hold fast to our development in Christ.

The Spirit of the Lord is upon me, because he hath
anointed me to preach the gospel to the poor; he
hath sent me to heal the brokenhearted, to preach

deliverance to the captives, and recovering of sight to the blind, to set at liberty them that are bruised. (Luke 4:18; emphasis added)

The same Spirit that empowered Jesus works in us today. We have been reborn of God's Spirit, the Holy Spirit.

> *The Spirit of the Lord GOD is upon me*; because the LORD hath anointed me to preach good tidings unto the meek; he hath sent me to bind up the brokenhearted, to proclaim liberty to the captives, and the opening of the prison to them that are bound. (Isaiah 61:1; emphasis added)

The Holy Spirit is able to apply His hand to our substance and develop God's intended Christlike image in us. He sets us free from our sinful simplicity to work us into His masterpiece.

Step 3: Flood the Clay with Water (Jesus)

Once the clay is securely attached to the wheel head, the potter literally floods the clay with water. The water acts as a lubricant between the clay and the potter's hands. This allows the potter to apply as much pressure to the clay as needed for minimal resistance without allowing it to stick to his or her hands. In the beginning of this process, the potter will have to apply water more often and more liberally.

The flooding of the clay closely symbolizes our water baptism and the transition point from which the old person is buried and the new person emerges. Jesus Himself set the pattern for us when He asked John to baptize Him.

Flooding the clay

This is the point at which the clay begins to cooperate within the hands of the potter. The remaining steps will eventually transform a simple ball of clay into an item with worth and function. The clay dies to itself and is transformed into a vessel worthy of the potter's touch.

> Then cometh Jesus from Galilee to Jordan unto John, to be baptized of him. But John forbad him, saying, I have need to be baptized of thee, and comest thou to me? And Jesus answering said unto him, Suffer it to be so now: for thus it becometh us to fulfill all righteousness. Then he suffered him. And Jesus, when he was baptized, went up straightway out of the water: and, lo, the heavens were opened unto him, and he saw the Spirit of God descending like a dove, and lighting upon him: And lo a voice from heaven, saying, This is my beloved Son, in whom I am well pleased. (Matthew 3:13–17)

Then was Jesus led up of the Spirit into the wilderness to be tempted of the devil. And when he had fasted forty days and forty nights, he was afterward an hungred. And when the tempter came to him, he said, If thou be the Son of God, command that these stones be made bread. But he answered and said, It is written, Man shall not live by bread alone, but by every word that proceedeth out of the mouth of God. (Matthew 4:1–4)

Again, this is the same Spirit, the Holy Spirit, who anointed the ministry of Jesus. Now, as we cooperate, He is free to do an anointed work in us.

As we allow Him to work, He brings us closer to Jesus, the author and finisher of our faith. The Holy Spirit wants us centered in Jesus and Jesus centered in us. If we resist, in the same way clay resists being centered, He honors our choice, and we will remain with a degree of wobble in our lives.Just as the water acts as a lubricant between the potter's hands and the clay, Jesus is the mediator between us and the hand of God. After all, Jesus said,

In the last day, that great day of the feast, Jesus stood and cried, saying, If any man thirst, let him come unto me, and drink.

He that believeth on me, as the scripture hath said, out of his belly shall flow rivers of living water. (John 7:37–38)

The clay, like us after salvation, is pliable but somewhat drier at the start of the process. As the clay is worked on the wheel and is continually drenched, it becomes more saturated, requiring less water to be worked into it. As the clay absorbs the water, it begins a change within the vital core of its body.

The same thing happens with us. Faith comes by hearing the Word of God not just once but frequently. The total source of our faith is found in Jesus Christ and the work He did on the cross for you and me.

> So then faith cometh by hearing, and hearing by the word of God. (Romans 10:17)

This process may take place quickly, or may be slow and gradual. Like clay, some of us adsorb a little faster and some a little slower. As the Word soaks into our minds, the Holy Spirit in us adsorbs the truth of it and causes it to settle in the hearts of our Spirit beings. A change in the vital core of who we are begins to take in us.

> And ye shall know the truth, and the truth shall make you free. (John 8:32)

It is the truth we know that sets us free. Being set free by faith in Jesus and what He did for us on the cross allows us to be worked by the hand of the potter. Freedom to be who God wants us to be is true freedom.

> Whom shall he teach knowledge? and whom shall he make to understand doctrine? Them that are

weaned from the milk, and drawn from the breasts. (Isaiah 28:9)

The doctrine of Jesus is truth. We need to go no further than Him to know and understand complete truth. As the Potter works the clay, shaping begins to take place. A lowly lump of clay gradually evolves into an anointed vessel.

> For precept must be upon precept, precept upon precept; line upon line, line upon line; here a little, and there a little. (Isaiah 28:10)

The wheel turns and turns, and then it turn and turns again. In the total process, hundreds and hundreds of turns take place. Faster in the beginning and then slower as the vessel beings to take shape and becomes more saturated.

Step 4: Wedging on the Wheel

In the initial working of the clay on the wheel, the speed needs to be fast. This stage takes the most strength the potter will need in the whole process. This process aligns the particles of clay. It is also the point at which the clay is still less saturated.

At the time of salvation, our spirits are made new in Christ. But our flesh is very dry and requires, like the clay, a deluge of the living Word to moisten our souls and soften our hearts to begin the process of aligning our spirits with His Word. We have mentioned this process before; it's called sanctification. Like the potter with the clay, the power of the Holy Spirit comes to work on and within us to align us with His Word and His will for our lives.

Wedging the clay on the wheel, and the next step, centering, are critical to the success of a skillfully and artfully produced pot.

Sanctification, by the washing of the Word, works our hearts and flesh into usable vessels that God conditions for His skillful and artful purposes. With the power of the Word applied to our lives, our flesh begins to take on God's nature to the degree that we yield. If our hearts and minds line up with the Spirit of truth, then sin nature will start to yield to God's intended designs and purposes for our lives.

Due to the speed of the wheel, centrifugal force causes a wobbling effect until the clay is perfectly centered. To the degree the clay is not centered, the process will be challenging. This step is necessary only when the potter senses additional work is needed in order to condition the clay for a better result.

> That every one of you should know how to possess his vessel in sanctification and honor. (1Thessalonians 4:4)

But we are bound to give thanks alway to God for you, brethren beloved of the Lord, because God hath from the beginning chosen you to salvation through sanctification of the Spirit and belief of the truth:

> Whereunto he called you by our gospel, to the obtaining of the glory of our Lord Jesus Christ. (2 Thessalonians 2:13–14)

Wedging clay on the wheel

The wheel-wedging process requires a pulling up and pushing down, a stretching and recompressing of the clay. This action assures a consistency in the texture and workability of the clay.

Like this process, God's chastisement seeks to stretch us and strengthen us in faith and trust by His touch and pull. He draws us closer to strengthen our resolve to yield totally to Him and cling to nothing of our former lives.

Resisting His hand and not yielding to His prompting can lead us to destruction. But there is good news. With repentance, as in Jeremiah 18, He can "make us again" a new vessel.

Step 5: Centering

Centering is the most critical step of all. If the lump of clay is not perfectly centered to the wheel head, the remaining steps will yield a vessel with a less than symmetrical shape. If the clay is off-center enough, even the best potter will have difficulty producing a vessel worthy of use.

When we yield to the hand of God, the Holy Spirit applies the Word to our lives and aligns us to it. When we yield to this process, the Word actually draws us closer to God and into the relationship He desires to have with us.

Just like clay on the wheel head, the closer we are to the center of God's will, the more of God's glory is projected through us. Our God, the ultimate potter, has the absolute and unfailing talent to produce a vessel of honor, no matter how corrupt the lump of clay. All it takes is a measure of faith in His ability to do it and plenty of His grace and mercy.

Centering the clay

When clay is not perfectly centered on the wheel, a wobble will be visible. Wobbles interfere with the hand of the potter in the same way sin interferes with God's ability to do His best work in us.

As the flesh begins to yield and mature in Jesus, sin, like wobbles, begins to disappear as we get centered into and by His Word. Like well-centered clay, our sin nature, by way of the Holy Spirit, eventually yields to our God-given designs and purposes. By the work of His hand, the flesh is remade into that usable vessel.

> I therefore, the prisoner of the Lord, beseech you that ye walk worthy of the vocation wherewith ye are called, With all lowliness and meekness, with longsuffering, forbearing one another in love; Endeavouring to keep the unity of the Spirit in the bond of peace.
>
> There is one body, and one Spirit, even as ye are called in one hope of your calling; One Lord, one faith, one baptism, One God and Father of all, who is above all, and through all, and in you all.
>
> But unto every one of us is given grace according to the measure of the gift of Christ. Wherefore he saith, When he ascended up on high, he led captivity captive, and gave gifts unto men.
>
> Now that he ascended, what is it but that he also descended first into the lower parts of the earth? He

that descended is the same also that ascended up far above all heavens, that he might fill all things. And he gave some, apostles; and some, prophets; and some, evangelists; and some, pastors and teachers; *For the perfecting of the saints, for the work of the ministry, for the edifying of the body of Christ: Till we all come in the unity of the faith, and of the knowledge of the Son of God, unto a perfect man, unto the measure of the stature of the fullness of Christ:* That we henceforth be no more children, tossed to and fro, and carried about with every wind of doctrine, by the sleight of men, and cunning craftiness, whereby they lie in wait to deceive; But speaking the truth in love, may grow up into him in all things, which is the head, even Christ. (Ephesians 4:1–15; emphasis added)

Step 6: Base Opening

Once it is well centered, the clay is ready to be opened. The potter will apply pressure in the center of the clay to make the interior opening. If the centering process has been done well, the clay will be easily opened. It will cooperate with the potter's guiding.

The width the interior is opened determines, in proportion, the exterior width of the base. The base of any vessel should be wide enough to allow it to stand firmly, without tipping over. At the same time, it should not be so wide as to distract the eye from its overall shape.

The base opening

This step parallels the foundation of our stance within God's purposes for our lives. It's the pattern on which He chooses to build us. Our faith, abilities, and environments produce the footing upon which we grow and develop into the image He desires.

> And Jesus answered and said unto him, Blessed art thou, Simon Barjona: for flesh and blood hath not revealed it unto thee, but my Father which is in heaven.
>
> And I say also unto thee, That thou art Peter, and upon this rock I will build my church; and the gates of hell shall not prevail against it. And I will give unto thee the keys of the kingdom of heaven: and whatsoever thou shalt bind on earth shall be bound in heaven: and whatsoever thou shalt loose on earth shall be loosed in heaven. (Matthew 16:17–19)

Jesus said, "Upon this rock I will build my church." He is the foundation, the cornerstone, the rock upon which we stand as believers. He is God. He is the Word of God. He invested Himself in humankind at creation and is humankind's way back to the Father.

> For by grace are ye saved through faith; and that not
> of yourselves: it is the gift of God. (Ephesians 2:8)

The knowledge of who He is and what He has done for us is the base upon which we stand spiritually.

Step 7: Pulling the Cylinder Up and Out

This is the most dramatic step in the entire process of forming a vessel. The potter and observers get to see the clay rise from a simple, low, bulky shape to a tall, slender cylinder that seems to defy God's law of gravity.

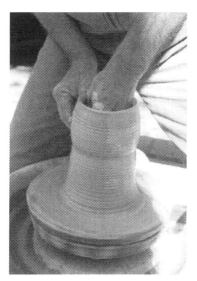

Photos of pulling a cylinder

Pulling the cylinder represents our growth in the knowledge of the Word and development of our relationship in Him by the direction of the Holy Spirit. The potter works with his or her fingertips directly opposite each other. One hand is inside the cylinder; the other on the outside. As the potter feels the clay spin between his or her fingers, the potter applies equal and consistent pressure from both sides, from bottom to top, and pulling upward.

Just as the potter does, our Father, in a loving way, applies

His conviction to our hearts in order to pull us upward and closer to Him. His hand, through the Holy Spirit, senses and guides our growth. When the Holy Spirit convicts us, He encourages repentance on our part and pulls us upward in growth and the knowledge of who He is.

As the cylinder rises, its walls get thinner, and the cylinder requires more delicate and skilled handling by the potter. This simulates the maturing and the shedding of self a believer goes through. The believer effectively turns him- or herself over, by faith, for the purpose and will of the Savior. The overall picture is one of God pulling humankind up toward their divine destiny as only God can perceive and do.

Hebrews 11:1 says, "Now faith is the substance of things hoped for, the evidence of things not seen." I have taken the liberty to use God's Word from Hebrews to expand on the analogy of the potter. With repetition, it goes like this.

> By the measure of *faith* given us *now* … we, the *substance*, place ourselves in the potter's hands to be formed into the *evidence* of our full potential, which is still *unseen.*

From this point on, the potter will use much less water because the clay will have absorbed much. It saturates and softens but needs to remain strong enough to stand.

So it is with us. As our relationship and fellowship mature, we become one with Christ in a greater way. We become more saturated in His Word and His Spirit. Our old hearts soften but remain firm enough in the knowledge of Him to stand against the forces of the world, the wiles of the devil, and the old sin nature that wants to continually rise up.

As mentioned in step 4, a well-centered vessel can deal with the centrifugal force applied to it. If we are well centered in Christ, we can stand strong in spite of the worldly forces placed against us.

Step 8: Shaping

In step 8, the Potter puts form and character into humans, the earthen vessels. Up to this point, we have a vertical cylinder overflowing with potential.

This step is the most beautiful of the whole process. When God pushes and pulls the vessel—a human—into the shape of his or her full potential, that person likewise displays the beauty of God's hand at work. It's at this point the shape forms into the beautiful vessel the Potter has imagined. As His Word says, "He has envisioned the beauty of who He wants us to be, since before creation."

> For God, who commanded the light to shine out of darkness, hath shined in our hearts, to give the light of the knowledge of the glory of God in the face of Jesus Christ.
>
> But *we have this treasure in earthen vessels*, that *the excellency of the power may be of God*, and not of us.
>
> We are troubled on every side, yet not distressed; we are perplexed, but not in despair; Persecuted, but not forsaken; cast down, but not destroyed; Always bearing about in the body the dying of the

Lord Jesus, that the life also of Jesus might be made manifest in our body. For we which live are alway delivered unto death for Jesus' sake, that the life also of Jesus might be made manifest in our mortal flesh. (2 Corinthians 4:6–11; emphasis added)

In the believer, we see the evidence of God's hand. Like the throw rings on a clay vessel, God leaves the traces of His work on each and every one of us.

On this earth, a potter applies to a clay vessel the skill and talent that God invested within him or her. But in the spiritual realm, God, the source of all skill and talent, applies His touch to the vessels, humankind. Have you felt His touch?

As described earlier, a potter works with his or her fingertips directly opposite each other. One hand is on the inside of the cylinder and the other on the outside. The potter's hands generally start low in the cylinder and push the clay outward, or perhaps inward, as desired while slowly pulling upward to the top of the spinning cylinder.

Remember, God works on us like a spinning cylinder, day after day, month after month, year after year.

When potters use their fingers inside a vessel to push the clay outward, the fingers outside the vessel guide the clay to the desired point. The process is simply reversed to push the clay inward.

God's inside hand pushes us outward into the knowledge of His Word, stretching us to meet our potential in Christ. At the same time, His hand on the outside provides support and builds trust in His perfect grace and mercy. His Spirit guides the whole process.

No matter which direction He is pushing you, remember on the opposite side is His hand of grace and mercy, asking you to trust in Him.

In this step, the potter will often stop and stand afar to evaluate how the shape has progressed. In our lives, we often feel God has walked away because we no longer feel His touch. As with the potter, perhaps He is evaluating the progress we have made. Are we beginning to reflect the shape of His Son?

The beauty of a vessel in progress is directly related to the skill, talent, and designed touch of the potter. He wants to see us reach our full potential in who we are and as who He is.

A shaped cylinder

Step 9: Trimming the Vessel

This is the final touch to finishing the raw clay pot. The purpose is to remove any excess clay that may detract from the finished shape. Trimming can take place at any step along the way as long as the clay has been centered. However, the mark of a good potter is a vessel that requires little to no trimming. This aspect is directly affected by how workable the clay is.

God's Word removes the excesses that accumulate in our flesh. He lovingly chastises us on the way to sanctification by trimming away the parts that distract from His design. He desires that we be in perfect balance with Him and at the same time be uniquely who He has designed us to be. The more we allow the Potter to do His work in us, the less we will need to be trimmed. If our trust in Him is sufficient, His talent will be observable. The mark of the one true Potter will be upon us.

Photo of trimming

> For the word of God is quick, and powerful, and sharper than any twoedged sword, piercing even to the dividing asunder of soul and spirit, and of the joints and marrow, and is a discerner of the thoughts and intents of the heart. (Hebrews 4:12)

Step 10: Drying

This next step is a function of time. The finished piece has to be placed in a safe, relatively dry place and protected so it does not dry too quickly. The slow drying allows the moisture to escape evenly throughout the pot. At the same time, the loss of moisture causes the raw clay to shrink uniformly, so it will be able to hold its shape. Any irregularities in the vessel at this point will be exaggerated once it's completely dry.

This step can be compared to the maturing process that takes place in a believer. Once we have reached a mature level of knowledge and faith in Jesus, His Word begins to "set up" in our hearts, solidifying who we are in Him. This firmness forms the basis of our abilities to stand against the elements of the world system and hold to the pattern of His distinctive design in us. Mature faith displays a tangible strength that lends confidence, joy, and trust to the believer, and at the same time becomes visible to those around him.

> If any man speak, let him speak as the oracles of God; if any man minister, let him do it as of the ability which God giveth: that God in all things may be glorified through Jesus Christ, to whom be praise and dominion forever and ever. Amen. (1 Peter 4:11)

Too often today we see mature believers, even pastors and teachers of the Word, caught publicly in sin. Through forgiveness, God the Potter can break that vessel down and start the remaking process, creating a humbler person.

> And the vessel that he made of clay was marred in the hand of the potter: *so he made it again another vessel*, as seemed good to the potter to make it. (Jeremiah 18:4; emphasis added)

As the clay shrinks, the molecules of the clay draw closer to each other. Shrinkage can be as much as 15 percent to 20 percent.

As John the Baptist stated," He must increase, but I must decrease" (John 3:30). As we decrease in ourselves (shrink to self), we increase in the strength He provides by faith. Our faith requires that we shrink in the confidence of what we can do. All our talents and abilities come directly from His hand at the point He designed us. Many people use that design to their benefit, become what the world calls successful, and never give God the credit. John said, "He must increase!" The basis of our design, the way He constructed you and me, is to glorify Him by giving Him the credit for all we have and accomplish.

Shrinkage of the clay continues in the next step as well. At this point, the vessel is still clay and can be broken down, dissolved, and completely reworked. We must never despair. No matter how far we have strayed from Him, His hand is always there to rework our "marred" selves.

Step 11: Firing

Once the vessel is completely dry and deemed worthy to be fired, the potter gathers enough pots to fill the kiln and begins the process of firing. Whether an electrical or a gas kiln, the temperature is raised very gradually over a period of several days. The slowness allows any remaining moisture to escape without turning to steam. If this should happen, the pot would explode, not only destroying itself, but perhaps other ones around it as well. As in the drying stage, the clay will shrink another 15 percent to 20 percent. The higher the temperature, the closer the molecules compress, ultimately forming a wall that becomes nonporous in certain clay bodies.

> Beloved, *think it not strange concerning the fiery trial which is to try you*, as though some strange thing happened unto you: But rejoice, inasmuch as ye are partakers of Christ's sufferings; that, when his glory shall be revealed, ye may be glad also with exceeding joy. (1 Peter 4:12–13; emphasis added)

Like the effect of a kiln on the clay, our permanency and cohesiveness come through the fiery trials of the world that only God can control. The Holy Spirit knows just how much heat we can take. He never allows more than our faith can handle. With passing time and varying circumstances, He allows the temperature to rise and strengthen us in Christ.

On the other hand, we may step away from His skillful hands and put ourselves in explosive situations, where the heat is too much for us to handle. Nonbelievers are more inclined to do this than are believers. However, the flesh we live in is still able to draw us into uncontrolled heat. This is the reason we must put stay in His hands, trust His expertise, and learn to follow the lead of His Spirit.

Like all the pots in the kiln, believers share a similarity in the work done by the Holy Spirit. He burns out impurities and leaves only the function, form, and beauty that reflect the image of its Creator.

As the kiln reaches the desired temperature, the potter in a gas-firing process often introduces different types of salts to coat the exposed surfaces of the vessels within. These salts liquefy on all surfaces within the kiln.

> Ye are the salt of the earth: but if the salt have lost his savour, wherewith shall it be salted? It is thenceforth good for nothing, but to be cast out, and to be trodden under foot of men. (Matthew 5:13)

The application of these salts creates a variation in color and texture on the surface of each pot. Because of the many unique variables used—temperature, type of fuel, humidity, loading of the kiln, salts used, and so on—firing produces a beauty in each piece that is difficult to replicate, even when all the steps are meticulously duplicated.

Our God wants us to be one of a kind, unique in every way!

> For every one shall be salted with fire, and every sacrifice shall be salted with salt. Salt is good: but if the salt have lost his saltness, wherewith will ye

season it? Have salt in yourselves, and have peace one with another. (Mark 9:49–50)

As the beauty and/or function of a salt-glazed pot ministers to the beholder, so are we to minister in Christ to each other and to those of the world around us.

Occasionally, a pot will have a piece of foreign matter hidden within its walls. Most of the time, this contamination can be spotted before the vessel is fired, but sometimes not. The good news is that nothing gets by the Holy Spirit. We must confess all sins and purposely hold on to the work He did for us and is doing in us.

Some of us hold on to sin for a period of time and then eventually confess it and ask forgiveness. If we hold on to sin and refuse to seek forgiveness, we place ourselves outside God's protection. We open the door to excessive and destructive heat in our lives. Remember, "If we confess our sins, he is faithful and just to forgive us our sins, and to cleanse us from all unrighteousness" (1 John 1:9).

If the contamination remains hidden during the firing, shrinkage from the extreme heat, which may reach 2,300 degrees, means the pot will likely not survive. It may shatter, crack, or warp beyond reasonable use. A good potter will not want to be known for having produced such a marred pot and will break it to an unrecognizable state. The only objects remaining after destruction are shards, which have no value other than to fill the holes in a gravel driveway.

Wherefore thus saith the Holy One of Israel, Because ye despise this word, and trust in oppression and perverseness, and stay thereon: Therefore this iniquity shall be to you as a breach ready to fall, swelling out in a high wall, whose breaking cometh suddenly at an instant. *And he shall break it as the breaking of the potters' vessel that is broken in pieces; he shall not spare: so that there shall not be found in the bursting of it a sherd* to take fire from the hearth, or to take water withal out of the pit. For thus saith the Lord GOD, the Holy One of Israel; In returning and rest shall ye be saved; in quietness and in confidence shall be your strength: and ye would not. (Isaiah 30:12-15 emphasis added)

When we trust in the Potter's hand, we allow Him to do a work that makes us usable vessels worthy of His intent. Only He knows why we have been designed in such a way. Why we have been born for such a day, and how we fit into His purpose for this day. When we experience the process of His hand upon us, it builds our faith, which in turn produces a quiet confidence and inner strength. Trust that hand!

CHAPTER 4 REVIEW

God has provided His Son and His Spirit so that we can be reworked from our dead spirits into His Spirit of eternal life. Throughout His Word, we find revelation of His desire to reclaim humankind in order to share true life, the life Adam had before he learned of the knowledge of good and evil. By faith, we can see the never-ending love God demonstrated with the sacrifice of His Son.

Clay on the potter's wheel closely parallels an image of the work He wants to do in us. We can see this by the conversation and image He presents to Jeremiah about the Hebrew people. By our faith, we are adopted into His family, giving Him the right to work with us as an extension of His chosen people.

God has selected each of us for a particular application based on His design, purpose, and destiny. The Holy Spirit teaches and coaches us through a process much like the potter who knows the clay and works it to its full potential. The design built into us is for honor and utility. He is no respecter of persons and extends His love to all.

As the potter looks at the clay and imagines its potential, our Creator looks at us and knows what He has already designed into us. He is more than able to rework us into His vision of our spiritual completeness. God knows our shortcomings so well that He can apply His grace and mercy in ways that turn us into material suitable for His use. By our obedience, we allow Him to apply His hands to our circumstances, pull us up, and form us into a most worthy vessel.

Our faith opens to us the knowledge of God's Word, line upon line, precept upon precept. It anchors us securely in our salvation. Faith allows God to begin a step-by-step process of growth. As our faith develops, it helps ensure that no matter how much force is exerted upon us by worldly circumstances or by His chastisement, we can hold fast to our faith.

A potter selects and pays for clay either monetarily or by the sweat of his or her brow. Our Master has redeemed us from the pit by the blood of His Son. You and I are priceless in the eyes of the Father. We should respond accordingly and allow Him to remake us in the image of His investment.

The firmness of a clay body is comparable to the firmness or strength of our faith. The clay's ability to absorb water can be compared to the degree of testing our faith can withstand with Christ in our lives.

In the beginning, the potter floods the clay with water, which acts as a lubricant between the clay and the potter's hands. This allows the potter to apply as much pressure to the clay as needed for minimal resistance without allowing it to stick to his or her hands. In the beginning of this process, the potter needs to apply water more often and more liberally. Flooding of the clay exemplifies our water baptism and the transition point from which the old person is buried and the new person emerges. It is also similar to our initial emersion into the Word, when we first come to faith in Jesus.

When the clay begins to cooperate within the hands of the potter, it's as if the clay dies to itself and can be transformed into whatever shape the potter chooses.

When we allow the Holy Spirit (teacher and coach) to do His

work, He always brings us closer to Jesus, the author and finisher of our faith. The Holy Spirit wants us to be centered in Jesus and Jesus centered in us. If we resist, He honors our choice.

> So then faith cometh by hearing, and hearing by the word of God. (Romans 10:17)

Complying with the process may take place quickly or be slow and gradual. Like clay, some of us adsorb a little faster and some a little slower. As the Word soaks into our minds, the Holy Spirit in us reveals its truth and causes it to settle in the heart.

> And ye shall know the truth, and the truth shall make you free. (John 8:32)

It is the truth we know that sets us free. Being set free by faith in Jesus and what He did for us on the cross allows us to be reworked personally by the hand of the potter. True freedom is becoming who God wants us to be.

The doctrine of Jesus is truth. We need to go no further than Him to know and understand complete truth.

As the potter works the clay, form begins to take place. A lowly lump of clay can gradually evolve into an anointed vessel.

At the time of salvation, our spirits are made new in Christ, but our flesh is very dry and, like the clay, requires a deluge of the living Word to moisten our souls and soften our hearts. We call this process sanctification. With the power of His Word applied to our lives, our flesh begins to take on God's nature to the degree that we yield.

Wheel-wedging is a process that requires a pulling up and

pushing down, a stretching and recompressing of the clay. Like this process, God's chastisement seeks to stretch us and strengthen us in faith and trust of His touch and pull. In doing so, He draws us closer, strengthening our resolves to yield to Him and let go of our former lives.

The lump of clay must be perfectly centered to the wheel head, or the following steps will yield a less functional and an unattractive vessel. When we yield to the process, it draws us into the relationship God desires to have with us.

Our God is the ultimate potter, with the absolute and unfailing talent to produce a vessel of honor, no matter how corrupt the lump of clay. All it takes from us is a measure of faith in His ability to do it.

As we yield and mature by being centered in Jesus, sin, like clay, wobbles on the wheel and begins to disappear. Similar to the wheel head, He is our foundation, the rock upon which we rest. He invested himself in humankind at creation and is humankind's only way back to the Father's original intent.

> For by grace are ye saved through faith; and that not
> of yourselves: it is the gift of God. (Ephesians 2:8)

Pulling the clay up and out is the most dramatic step in the entire process of forming a vessel. The potter and observers get to see the clay rise from a simple, low, bulky shape to a tall, slender cylinder that seems to defy God's law of gravity.

The potter works with his or her fingertips directly opposite each other. One hand is inside the cylinder, and the other is on the outside. As the potter feels the clay spin between his or her fingers, the potter consistently applies equal pressure from both sides, from the bottom to the top while pulling upward.

In real life, we often have to repeat the learning process before our understanding sets in. The clay on the wheel head spins hundreds of times before the task is complete. So too the Father, with His loving Spirit, applies conviction to our hearts and pulls us up and closer to Himself.

As the cylinder rises, its walls get thinner, requiring a more delicate handling by the potter. The Holy Spirit facilitates that special touch and creates in us a maturity by the shedding of self. The believer turns him- or herself over, by faith, to the purpose and will of the Savior. God's desire is to put His form and character back into us, the earthen vessels.

As our relationship matures in Christ, we become more saturated in His Word. Our new hearts soften a bit yet remain firm enough to stand against the world, evil, and our old sin nature that continually wants to rise up.

The most beautiful step of the whole process is when God, with His own hands, pushes and pulls us into the shape of our full potential. No matter which direction He is pushing you, remember that on the opposite side is His hand in grace and mercy asking you to trust Him.

Trimming can take place at any step in the process as long as the clay has been well centered. The mark of a good potter is a vessel that requires little to no removal of excess clay that will detract from the finished vessel. To a believer, God's Word can remove excesses that accumulate in our flesh. He lovingly chastises us in the process of sanctification, trimming away extremes that are a distraction to His design. Mature faith displays the balance and symmetry of God that others can see.

The potter deals with the shrinkage of the clay throughout the process of drying and firing. Our faith requires that we shrink in the confidence of what we can do. All our talents and abilities come directly from His hand. As we decrease in ourselves (shrink to self), we increase in the strength of who He is.

Many people become what the world calls successful and never give God the credit. John said, "He must increase!" (John 3:30a) The basis of our design is to glorify and give Him credit for all He accomplishes in us.

We must never despair. No matter how far we have strayed from Him, His hand is always there. Clay can always be broken down, dissolved, and completely reworked. Like the effect of a kiln on clay, our permanency and cohesiveness come through fiery trials of the world. The Potter has control of that too. The Holy Spirit knows just how much heat we can take. He never allows more than our faith can handle. With passing time and varying circumstances, He allows the temperature to rise and strengthen us in Christ.

He burns out impurities in our lives, leaving only function, form, and beauty to reveal the image of our Creator. As the beauty and function of a vessel ministers to the beholder, so are we to minister to each other and those of the world, as did Christ.

Hebrews 11:1 says, "Now faith is the substance of things hoped for, the evidence of things not seen."

My hope is that you come away from God's analogy with a better understanding and perhaps a better visual image of how

God wants to work with His hand upon you. We are His material of choice.

By the measure of faith given us now, we, the substance, place ourselves in the Potter's hands to be formed into the evidence of our full potential, which is still unseen. In the believer, we see evidence of God's hand. Like throw rings on a clay vessel, He leaves the heavenly traces of His touch on every believer.

Many of us sing, "You are the potter, I am the clay. Mold me and make me, this is what I pray."

ABOUT THE AUTHOR

David Romero is a believer in Jesus Christ for more than forty years. His formal education is in three-dimensional design. He is enthralled with wheel-thrown pottery and has spent more than twenty years working with it. In the process of spiritual growth and skill development on the wheel, God revealed to him the analogy illustrated in this book. It is one of tremendous parallel between the potter, God, and the clay, man.

Printed in the United States
By Bookmasters